MAY 1 9 1998

MAY 1 9 1998

Wind
in My Pocket

Copyright © 1990 Ellen Bryan Obed (text)
Shawn Steffler (illustrations)

Canadian Cataloguing in Publication Data

Obed, Ellen Bryan, 1944-

    Wind in my pocket

    Poems.
    ISBN 0-920911-74-9

I. Steffler, Shawn, 1950-. II. Title.

PS8579.B42W56 1989   jC811'.54   C89-098640-1
PZ8.3.033Wi 1989

Breakwater Books
100 Water Street
P.O. Box 2188
St. John's, Newfoundland, Canada
A1C 6E6

The Publisher acknowledges the assistance of The Canada Council which has helped make this publication possible.

The Publisher acknowledges the financial contribution of the Cultural Affairs Division of the Department of Municipal and Provincial Affairs, Government of Newfoundland and Labrador, which has helped make this publication possible.

Wind in My Pocket

Ellen Bryan Obed
illustrations by Shawn Steffler

for the children of
Newfoundland
Labrador
and the Quebec North Shore

and for my uncle
Robert A. Bryan
who first introduced me to them

Tell me of sun,
Sing me of snow,
Read me of wind,
Then I will go.

Ribbon Seller's Song

Ribbons, ribbons, plenty of ribbons!
Will anyone buy from me
    Ribbons of sunlight,
    Ribbons of seaweed,
Ribbons of bark from the tree?

Ribbons, ribbons, I sell ribbons.
Will anyone stop to buy
    Ribbons of rootlets,
    Ribbons of rainbows,
Ribbons of cloud from the sky?

Grass Song

Witchgrass, stitchgrass, in-the-roadside-ditch grass;
Junegrass, strewn grass, waving-on-the-dune grass;
    Everywhere I pass, grass. Everywhere I see

Bluegrass, new grass, wet-with-morning-dew grass;
Sniff grass, stiff grass, growing-on-the-cliff grass;
    Everywhere I pass, grass. Everywhere I see

Fox-tail, squirrel-tail, standing-brown-and-stale grass;
Barley, timothy, tickles-on-the-knee grass;
    Everywhere I pass, grass. Everywhere I see

Clump grass, stump grass, even-in-the-dump grass;
Moose grass, goose grass, anyone can use grass;
Sweet grass, peat grass—we can even EAT grass!
    Everywhere I pass, grass—and grasses pass me!

The River

The river is a long and quiet place to be,
Wide and contented, moving to the sea.
Of slow tide and dark bank and tired stone—
Far from its white streams, deep and alone.
Wide and contented, moving to the sea;
The river is a long and quiet place to be.

Rhubarb

Long the fishing place abandoned,
Long the houses gray and still,
Long the gravestones dim and leaning,
But the rhubarb by the hill
Straight and high as if the pickers
Soon would pull the stalks aside—
Some for sauce and some for puddings,
Some for summer supper pies.

Let's Sing of Strawberries

Let's sing of strawberries
    for shortcake and pie
when there's a fragrant breeze
    and a ripening sky.

Let's walk to the patch
    that hides in the hay
with baskets and dippers
    for a strawberry day.

We'll bend in the grasses
    until the evening comes;
then with strawberry faces
    and strawberry thumbs,

We'll go home with strawberries
    for shortcake and pie
as the strawberry sun
    stains a strawberry sky.

Pals

Charles is my pal,
I'm his chum.
But Charles chews cherries
And I chew gum.

Charles plays checkers,
I like to chat.
Charles chases chipmunks,
I chase the cat.

Charles has chickens,
I keep bees.
Charles likes chips,
I choose cheese.

Charles chews cherries,
I chew gum.
But Charles is my pal
And I'm his chum.

Wind Song

"When one is in love with the Wind, Mother,
When one cannot sleep for its blow,
When all one can feel are its arms, Mother;
When one loves the Wind, does it know?

Yes, I am in love with the Wind, Mother,
And all I can hear or can see
Or feel or want is the Wind, Mother;
Do you think the Wind also loves me?"

There Once Was a Man Down the Bay

There once was a man down the bay
Who wanted black hair—not gray—
    So he decided to use
    Some blackberry juice,
But his hair became purple that day.

Now this gentleman man was so vain
That none dared to mention the stain
    That ran down his cheeks
    In purplish streaks
Whenever it started to rain.

"When Ye Goes"

"Winter will come when ye goes, Miss,
Though spring has just gone away.
The current is cold from the floes, Miss,
And snow's on the hills in the bay.

The sky will git gray as the rocks, Miss;
The dogs will be mocking the blow
Of the wind and asking it loud, Miss,
When it's bringing its bullwhips of snow.

When ye goes away to your place, Miss,
Do ye think o' the summer again?
When winter is long in our land, Miss,
We talks o' the sound o' the plane."

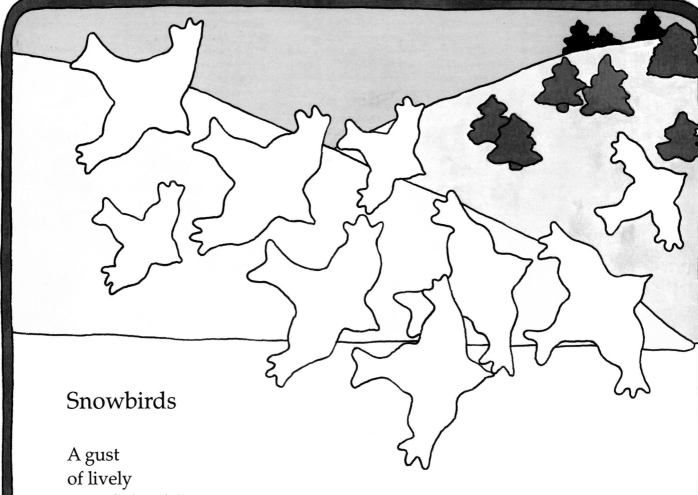

Snowbirds

A gust
of lively
snowflakes fell.
(I thought
that Winter
knew them well.)
But when
they rose
in quickest flight,
somehow
something
wasn't right.

Upon the wind,
upon the sky,
the snowbirds
make another try.

Winter Journey

In goose-down fields
        we leave our tracks
while black-crow cliffs
        look down our backs.
Over porcupine hills
        we make our way
to the red fox sun
        on the side of day.

Arctic Fox

White as the white of snow on snow,
He curls in the whirls of the arctic blow;
We can't see him sleep and can't see him go—
White as the white of snow on snow.

Blizzard

The night is so wild with snow
I fear the world might lose its way
And fall back into yesterday,
Or race so fast instead
Tumble several days ahead.
And I would be left standing by
In a house of wind with a roof of sky!

Winter Choice

This shovel,
That shovel,
Which one shall I chose
to shovel
shining chunks of snow
from the shingles
of my roof?

This shovel,
That shovel,
I shall put them back.
I can't shovel
chunks of snow
from my shingles
on my shack.

This wind,
That wind,
I shall ask instead,
"Please blow
the chunks of snow
from the shingles
on my shed."

When

When will the ice break up in the north?
When will the boats whish up to the wharf?
When will the white of snow disappear?
When will the geese whistle green the year?
When will the whale whirl up the sea?
When will the wind whisper warm to me?

The Skate

The ice is thick.
The ice is thin.
If I skate,
Will I fall in?

Temperature down,
Sun up high;
Spiral and spin,
I think I'll try.

Thick is thick.
Thin is thin—
When I went out,
I went in!

Sky Carver

Gently the sun
with steady eye
whittled at winter
from the sky.

Deeper she cut
with sharpened ray
as pieces of winter
fell away.

Warmly she held
it up when done,
"This is my carving called Spring,"
said the Sun.

The White Ships

No wife leans to the window glass;
No eager children wait the bow;
No dogs wake hungry on the rocks
To meet the ships that enter now.

They come—the white ships of the spring—
Built far north of the Labrador.
The Sea, their captain, brings them in
To sun and quiet tide, their shore.

Spring Thought

Little ones upon the bough,
Do they think of autumn now
In the infancy of spring?
Do the petals feel their seed?
Do the birds know they have wings,
Or do they think of other things?

The Robin Sang

The robin sang
with his red breast high.
He sang loud and late
to the red-breast sky.

The robin sang
'til the spruce was black.
He sang to the sky
with its cloud-feathered back.

The robin was still
when the sky was gone.
Dark in the spruce,
he sat alone.

The robin sang
with his red breast high
when early again
came the red-breast sky.

Wind in My Pocket

With wind in my pocket up from the sea
    and a cloud from the sky to wear,
With a bundle of sun tucked under my arm
    and ribbons of rain in my hair,
I walked to a bend in the afternoon
    for a friend who was waiting there.